Looney Limericks

Selected and Edited by
FRANK JACOBS

Illustrated by
LARRY DASTE

DOVER PUBLICATIONS, INC.
Mineola, New York

Bibliographical Note

Looney Limericks is a new work, first published by Dover Publications, Inc., in 1999.

International Standard Book Number: 0-486-40615-6

Manufactured in the United States of America
Dover Publications, Inc., 31 East 2nd Street, Mineola, N.Y. 11501

What's a Limerick?

What's a limerick? It's a five-line poem that tells you a quick story all in rhyme.

If you've never seen one, then you're in for a treat. Limericks are fun to read, easy to memorize, and great to share with your friends.

Here are sixty limericks—some old, some new, but all of them chosen for their looniness. They probably won't change your life, although—

There once was a man mean and proud
Who never would smile, so he vowed;
    He then took a look
    At this limerick book,
And guess what! He's now laughing out loud.

                        Frank Jacobs

There was a young man of Bengal
Who went to a masquerade ball;
   He dressed, just for fun,
   As a hamburger bun,
And a dog ate him up in the hall.

There was an old fellow named Green
Who grew so abnormally lean,
    And flat, and compressed,
    That his back touched his chest,
And sideways he couldn't be seen.

A mouse in her room woke Miss Dowd;
She was frightened and screamed very loud;
   Then a happy thought hit her—
   To scare off the critter,
She sat up in bed and meowed.

A tutor who tooted the flute
Tried to tutor two tooters to toot;
    Said the two to the tutor,
    "Is it harder to toot or
To tutor two tooters to toot?"

A man dining out in Peru
Found a rather large mouse in his stew;
   Said the waiter, "Don't shout
   And wave it about
Or the rest will be wanting one too!"

There was a young lady of Kent
Whose nose was most awfully bent;
    One day, I suppose,
    She followed her nose,
For no one knew which way she went.

There was an old man of Blackheath,
Who sat on his set of false teeth.
   Said he, with a start,
    "O Lord, bless my heart!
I've bitten myself underneath!"

A very large woman named Kate
Is six hundred pounds overweight;
   On an overseas trip
   She's transported by ship
In a wooden container marked "Freight."

Frank Jacobs

There once was a knowing raccoon
Who didn't believe in the moon;
  "Every month—don't you see?
  There's a new one," said he;
No *real* moon could wear out so soon!"

Mary Mapes Dodge

There was an old man with a beard
Who said, "It is just as I feared!
   Two owls and a hen,
   Four larks and a wren,
Have all built their nests in my beard!"

Edward Lear

There was a young farmer of Leeds,
Who swallowed six packets of seeds;
   It soon came to pass
   He was covered with grass,
And he couldn't sit down for the weeds.

In the forest an old armadillo
Took a nap 'neath a large weeping willow;
   Just a moment ago
   He learned to his woe
That a porcupine's not a good pillow.

Frank Jacobs

There was a young woman from Niger
Who smiled and rode out on a tiger;
   They returned from the ride
   With the lady inside
And a smile on the face of the tiger.

A cannibal living in France
Ate an uncle and two of his aunts,
  A cow and her calf,
  An ox and a half,
And now he can't button his pants.

There once was a skunk in the dell
Who hated all people, they tell;
  "Human beings," he said,
  Always fill me with dread,
Plus they give off that terrible smell!"

Frank Jacobs

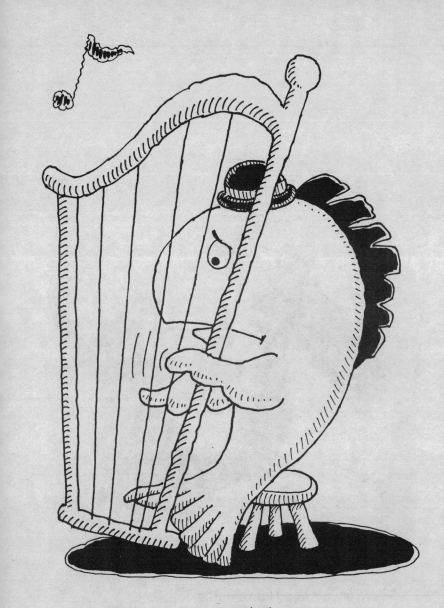

There once was a musical carp
Who wanted to play on a harp;
   But we sadly report
   That his fin was so short
That he couldn't reach up to C sharp.

There once was a silly young ape
Who gave up his skin for a cape;
   Now he swings through the trees,
   All exposed to the breeze,
Which leaves him in very bad shape.

A lion whose manners weren't nice
Played Monopoly with two white mice;
   After losing, he roared,
   Then devoured the board,
Marvin Gardens, both mice and the dice.

Frank Jacobs

There once was a hungry old leopard
Who brought home a skinny young shepherd;
  Said the leopard, "I feel
  That you'll make a good meal
Once you're properly salted and peppered."

There was a young farmer of Leeds,
And simple indeed were his needs;
    Said he, "I won't toil
    Growing things in the soil—
I'll just eat the packets of seeds."

There were three little birds in the wood
Who sang hymns any time that they could;
   What the words were about
   They could never make out,
But they felt it was doing them good.

A dashing young spotted hyena
Made a date with an aardvark named Lena;
 "Let's go dancing," said he;
 "Sounds like fun," answered she,
But I won't do that darned macarena!"

Frank Jacobs

Once a grasshopper (food being scant)
Begged an ant some assistance to grant;
   But the ant shook his head;
   "I can't help you," he said,
"It's an uncle you need, not an ant."

Oliver Herford

A barber who lived in Batavia
Was known for his fearless behavia;
  When a giant brown bear
  Took a seat in the chair,
Said the barber, "No way will I shavia."

A careless zookeeper named Blake
Fell into a tropical lake;
   Said a fat alligator
   A few minutes later,
"Not bad, but I still prefer steak."

There was a strange man from Dundee
Who claimed he was Francis Scott Key;
   When his friends said, "No way!"
   He replied, "That's okay—
As of now I am Robert E. Lee."

Frank Jacobs

There was an old man of Khartoum
Who kept two tame sheep in his room;
   He said, "They remind me
    Of one left behind me;
I just can't remember of whom."

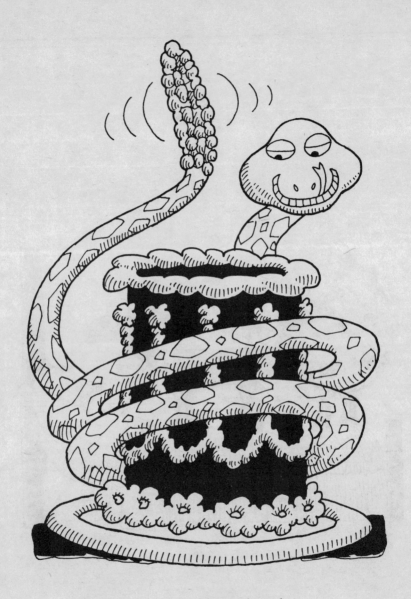

There once was a big rattlesnake
Who purchased a chocolate cake;
   When they said, " 'Twould be nice
    If you gave us a slice,"
He replied, "That would be a mistake."

There was a young man from the city
Who met what he thought was a kitty;
　　He gave it a pat
　　And said, "Nice little cat";
Just look at him now—what a pity!

Little Jimmy, who barely was three,
Made a nest in the bough of a tree;
    When his dad asked him why,
    He replied with a sigh,
"There was nothing I liked on TV."

Frank Jacobs

There once was a lady from Ealing
Who had a peculiar feeling
   That she now was a fly
   And wanted to try
To walk upside down on the ceiling.

There was a young man of St. Kitts
Who was very much troubled with fits;
   The eclipse of the moon
    Threw him into a swoon;
Soon he tumbled and broke into bits.

There was a young prince in Bombay
Who always would have his own way;
   He pampered his horses
    On five or six courses,
Himself eating nothing but hay.

Walter Parke

There once was a man who said, "Oh,
Please, good Mr. Bear, let me go!
    Don't you think that you can?"
    The bear looked at the man
And calmly replied, "Heavens, no."

To an eagle declared a giraffe,
"Soon I'll fly up and tear you in half";
   Said the eagle, up high,
    "Okay, give it a try—
It's been years since I've had a good laugh."
Frank Jacobs

I'd rather have fingers than toes;
I'd rather have ears than a nose;
  And as for my hair,
  I'm glad it's still there;
I'll be awfully sad when it goes.

Gelett Burgess

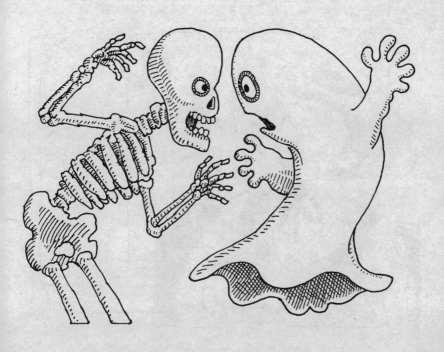

A ghost in the town of Khartoum
Asked a skeleton up to his room;
    They spent the whole night
    In the eeriest fight
As to who should be frightened of whom.

There was, in the village of Patton,
A man who at church kept his hat on;
   "If I wake up," he said,
   With my hat on my head,
I'll know that it hasn't been sat on."

There was an old lady of Rye
Who was baked by mistake in a pie;
   To the household's disgust
   She emerged through the crust
And exclaimed with a yawn, "Where am I?"

There was an old man in a barge,
Whose nose was exceedingly large;
　　But in fishing by night,
　　It supported a light,
Which helped that old man in a barge.

Edward Lear

There was a composer named Bong
Who composed a new popular song;
    It was simply the croon
    Of a lovesick baboon,
With occasional thumps on the gong.

There was an old man of Nantucket
Who kept all his cash in a bucket;
   But his daughter, named Nan,
   Ran away with a man,
And as for the bucket, Nantucket.

I wish that my room had a floor;
I don't care so much for a door,
  But this walking around
  Without touching the ground
Is getting to be quite a bore!

Gelett Burgess

There was a young lady of Crete,
Who was so exceedingly neat,
   When she got out of bed,
   She stood on her head
To make sure of not soiling her feet.

A glutton who lived on the Rhine
When asked at what time he would dine,
   Replied, "At eleven,
    Four, six, three and seven,
And eight and a quarter to nine."

There was an old man of Tarentum
Who gnashed his false teeth till he bent 'em;
    When asked what they cost
    And how much he had lost,
He replied, "I don't know—I just rent 'em."

A centipede known as Old Pete
Bought shoes custom-made for his feet;
   Said he, "There's a chance
   I might go to a dance,
And I must have my outfit complete."

There once was a provident puffin
Who ate all the fish he could stuff in;
   Said he, " 'Tis my plan
   To eat when I can—
When there's nuffin' to eat I eat nuffin.' "

Oliver Herford

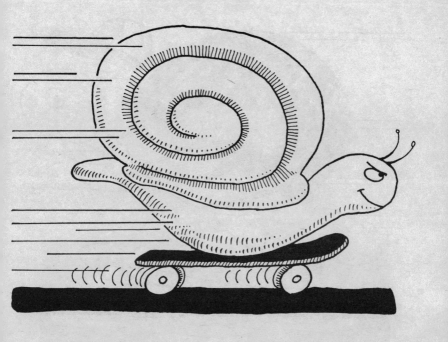

Said the snail to the tortoise: "You may
Find it hard to believe what I say;
   You will think it absurd,
   But I give you my word,
They fined me for speeding today."

Oliver Herford

"Well, well," said the tortoise. "Dear me!
How defective your motor must be!
    Though I speed ev'ry day,
    Not a fine do I pay;
The police cannot catch me, you see."

Oliver Herford

There once were two cats of Kilkenny;
Each thought there was one cat too many;
    So they fought paw to paw
    And they scratched claw to claw,
Till instead of two cats there weren't any.

A cheerful old bear at the zoo
Could always find something to do;
    When it bored him to go
    On a walk to and fro,
He reversed it, and walked fro and to.

There was a young girl of Manilla,
So fond of ice cream vanilla,
　　That sad to relate
　　Though you piled up her plate,
'Twas impossible ever to fill her.

There was a young man from Elora,
Who married a girl called Lenora,
   But he had not been wed
   Very long till he said,
"Oh, drat it! I've married a snorer!"

A king who began on his reign,
Exclaimed with a feeling of pain,
   "Though I'm legally heir,
    No one seems to care
That I haven't been born with a brain."

There was a young fellow who sat
Quite thoughtlessly flat on his hat.
   He reposed there a while
   And so altered its style,
That he uses it now for a mat.

An oyster from Kalamazoo
Confessed he was feeling quite blue.
  "For," says he, "as a rule,
   When the weather turns cool,
I invariably get in a stew!"

A certain young woman named Hannah
Slipped down on a piece of banana;
   She shrieked and oh, my'd,
   And more stars she spied
Than belong to the star-spangled banner.

There was an old man on whose nose
Most birds of the air could repose
   But they all flew away
   At the closing of day,
Which relieved that old man and his nose.

                   Edward Lear

There was a young lady whose chin
Resembled the point of a pin;
   So she had it made sharp,
   And purchased a harp,
And played several tunes with her chin.

Edward Lear